"*Contemplation is no pain killer*"

~ Thomas Merton

Also by L. Ward Abel

The Width of Here (Silver Bow Publishing)
Peach Box and Verge (Little Poem Press)
Jonesing for Byzantium (UKA Press)
The Heat of Blooming (Pudding House Press)
Torn Sky Bleeding Blue (Erbacce Press)
Cousins Over Colder Fields (Finishing Line Press)
American Bruise (Parallel Press)
Roseorange (Flutter Press)
Little Town gods (Folded Word Press)
A Jerusalem of Ponds (Erbacce Press)
Digby Roundabout (Kelsay Books)
The Rainflock Sings Again (Unsolicited Press)
Floodlit (Beakful Press)

Green Shoulders

New and Selected Poems
2003 - 2023

by

L. Ward Abel

720 – Sixth Street, Box # 5
New Westminster, BC
V3C 3C5   CANADA

Title: Green Shoulders
Author: L. Ward Abel
Cover Photo: by L. Ward Abel
Layout and Cover Design: Candice James
Editor: Candice James

All rights reserved including the right to reproduce or translate this book or any portions thereof, in any form without the permission of the publisher. Except for the use of short passages for review purposes, no part of this book may be reproduced, in part or in whole, or transmitted in any form or by any means, electronically or mechanically, including photocopying, recording, or any information or storage retrieval system without prior permission in writing from the publisher or a licence from the Canadian Copyright Collective Agency (Access Copyright).

www.silverbowpublishing.com
info@silverbowpublishing.com
ISBN: 9781774032756 print book
ISBN: 9781774032763 e book
© Silver Bow Publishing 2023

Library and Archives Canada Cataloguing in Publication

Title: Green shoulders / by L. Ward Abel.
Names: Abel, L. Ward, author.
Description: Poems.
Identifiers: Canadiana (print) 20230522114 | Canadiana (ebook) 20230522130 | ISBN 9781774032756 (softcover) | ISBN 9781774032763 (Kindle)
Classification: LCC PS3601.B45 G73 2023 | DDC 811/.6—dc23

L. Ward Abel

"Selected Poems" in this collection are taken from the following previous collections and chapbooks by the poet, as designated herein:

Peach Box and Verge (Little Poem Press, 2003)
Jonesing for Byzantium (UKA Press, 2006)
The Heat of Blooming (Pudding House Press, 2008)
Torn Sky Bleeding Blue (Erbacce Press, 2010)
American Bruise (Parallel Press, 2012)
Cousins Over Colder Fields (Finishing Line Press, 2013)
Roseorange (Flutter Press, 2013)
Little Town gods (Folded Word Press, 2016)
A Jerusalem of Ponds (Erbacce Press, 2016)
Digby Roundabout (Kelsay Books, 2017)
The Rainflock Sings Again (Unsolicited Press, 2019)
Floodlit (Beakful, 2019)
The Width of Here (Silver Bow, 2021)

The "New Poems" in this collection that have previously appeared in other publications are as follows:
"The Pond is Low," "The Unused Gate"—Meat for Tea
"The Planets," "Tonnage on the Rivers"—Main Street Rag
"Yellow Butterflies Return"—Reformed Journal
"The Light that Travels"—Young Ravens Literary Review
"Sunlight from a high window"—Dipity
"Still"—Whisky Blot
"So Change the Doves"—Whimperbang
"Kneel the Cattle"—Flyover Country
"The Good and the Gone-to-Seed"—Beir Bua
"A Dove's on the Roof," "Matte," "Shake and Flash" — Unconventional Courier
"Sunrise, Late Winter"—Amsterdam Review
"That Massif in the Room"—Hyacinth Review
"More Like Breathing Than Rain," "The Usual Path of Cranes"—Green Silk Journal
"Cartographer"—Dashboard Horus

Green Shoulders

Table of Contents

Selected Poems / 11

Hilltop Road / 13
August She Flies on By / 15
Water Meadow / 16
My Very Late Grandfather / 18
Gray Highway / 19
This Valley Is Full of Water / 20
Bestridden / 21
Bloomfield / 22
Flood the Intersection with Bright, Bright Light / 23
The Ridgeline That Would Be Pine Mountain / 24
Even Nixon Could Change a Tire / 27
Luxeme / 28
Things Left Behind / 29
Rainy Season June / 30
Growing Season / 31
The Heat of Blooming / 32
Thomaston / 33
Cope / 34
Receiving Line / 35
We Met in The Rothko Chapel / 36
Arthur's Seat at Night / 37
Gather Me / 38
Leaves / 39
Lizella / 40
Something Good Has Come from Rotting / 41
Dead / 42
Birds Won't Nest in The Sky / 43
The Viewing / 44
Ray with Tess / 45
Crazy / 46
Along the River Rd. / 47
Ocmulgee Trio / 48
Griffin / 50
Monticello / 51
Wild Ravine / 52
The Salmon / 53

Up Missouri / 54
Orson Welles Was a Liar / 55
Bill Evans / 56
It Rained on Resurrection Day / 57
Breaks / 58
On This Side / 59
In A Clearing a Shack / 60
Like Kim Novak in Vertigo / 61
Low Water / 62
Knowledge of Rooms / 63
War / 64
Stork / 65
Macon 1967 / 66
Anxiety / 67
The Killdeer Wheel / 68
Oconee / 69
Funeral Rd. / 70
Near the Lebanon / 71
The Road to Hamilton / 72
Ghost Over Woods / 73
Haralson / 74
Upriver Cloud to Cloud / 75
In an Effort to Fly / 76
Move / 77
Mornings at My Angkor Wat / 78
Shallows Walking / 79
The Return / 80
Where the Five Counties Meet / 81
A Great Wheel Thunders / 82
Breathing Through Planks / 83
Water Lily / 84
The Leaving Part / 85
John Bell Hood / 86
Floridita / 87
The Torn Screen / 88
The Flats / 89
Storm Over Three Forks / 90
Smarr / 91
Tranquility Base / 92
A Sky Wide Russet Flock Ascending / 93

Your Breathing / 94
Unanimity / 95
All of Our Living / 96
Miller's Thumb / 97
Between Butler and Columbus / 98
Halo / 99
Portion / 100
Conversation with Rothko / 101

New Poems 2022-2023 / 103

After A Few Wet Months / 105
Sunrise Late Winter / 106
Pastoral January / 107
Slow Burn Sky / 108
Beyond the Fire Pit / 109
Current / 110
Tonnage on the Rivers / 111
Kneel the Cattle / 112
Older Fields / 113
Almost Full Moon Through Branches / 114
Still / 115
The Usual Path of Cranes / 116
Another Springing Forth / 117
The Ibis Returns / 118
Yellow Butterflies Return / 119
A Birdshadow Drones This Low Country / 120
Above and Over / 121
The Light that Travels / 122
The Planets / 123
Sunlight From a High Window / 124
A Dove's on the Roof / 125
So Change the Doves / 126
That Massif in the Room / 127
Where I Planted Trees / 128
The World Breathes Out / 129
Shake and Flash / 130
Along the Line / 131
The Pond is Low / 132
How A Painting Sings the Rainshadow Song / 133

More Like Breathing Than Rain / 134
Matte / 135
The Unused Gate / 136
There Since One of The Wars / 137
The Good and The Gone to Seed / 138
Cartographer / 139
Wednesday / 140
A Storm Out to the East / 141

Selected Poems

Green Shoulders

Peace Box and Verge (2003)

Hilltop Road

Hilltop Road is not really a road at all
more like a street three-quarter to a mile long
with houses close along its short relief
all built in the sixties
twelve hundred to fifteen hundred square feet
red brick yellowish brick splits and ranches
trees up to the slope.

I lived here until I was seven
played in these civil war riddled woods
burned my handbrakes going down
to the bottomless pavement
where Tony Henry played me my first records
and crawfish filled the creek
where granddaddy built a block playhouse
and my mother planted magnolia.

Tonight I went down the neighborhood
coming back from buying shoelaces
the sky was pink and blue
clouds those colors and more yet
looking deceptively permanent.

My old house sat under dusk then
crescent moon at angle
reassuring
disrepair to some degree went unnoticed
because this was chock full
of those little sparks in your gut
that pass for memory
like tastes and smells and laughter and crying
like all those old gone relations
reclined after some big meal
out in the den
with NFL on a black and white

not far from the curb
under
our
middle class
banyan.

August She Flies on By

August she flies on by,
always preceding
or in a wake,
hot nasty pungent
somewhat like
the dumpster parking lot corner
without shade
from anything direct,
or like
a stripper post-prime
her microwaved blooms
as evidence only
of cool spring evenings long gone
and yet to come--
but for someone else.
I felt sorry for her
as September was near
that no one
had placed a floral
out on Zebulon Road
near the county line,
where
so many of her kind
were now
just
greasy spots.

Water-Meadow

Saw w. b. yeats
on the way home today
there ahead about
a quarter mile and closing

didn't seem
surprised to see me
like he knew my name
his left lens obscure

a cold wind blew up
from the water-meadow
sensed his trouble
risen from springs

asking solamente
complected questions
jonesing for byzantium yet
and off the right-of-way

lake isles in the sky
that little valley those garden walls
sudden nervous indifference directed
my inferiority near

closer
along the road
worn winter clothing
fifty degrees of intense

somehow a smile from him though
to the doppler machine
window-glass riverish
deep as i passed

deep as i passed
tipped gulfward pane down

open to word
relented wet

then gone rearview
but signs blown into rippling velvet
pre printed bolted silken
butler's jabs.

My Very Late Grandfather

The conversation with Grandfather
was a dream
I had
just before dawn today,
noticing his full head of gray hair
not being patched with matrilineal scalp
like mine.
He grinned as if teasing, without words
looked above my eyeline, and then beyond,
implying
a big-picture conclusion
that I too would share,
chuckling
a spring shower of comfort upon me;
unison
with him
now breaks
my rising.

Jonesing for Byzantium **(2006)**

Gray Highway

stretches almost due north
from Macon
into Jones County and to its seat
also named Gray.
A double-meaning permeates
that pavement
devoid of color
melancholy,
always the quiet ride.

It was the path my grandfather drove
taking me and my brother up
to Lake Sinclair,
past fruit groves
and massive stands of pine,
when summer had real meaning
and distinguished itself
from all other seasons.

Now the highway is indeed
a gray wand that conjures the dead
cutting through white and red clay,
green fields,
and the blue eyes
of grandfather's
evaporation.

This Valley Is Full Of Water

This valley is full of water
and fence-lines. Sometimes along the fences
trees will begin to grow,
as no one can get to them
under the wire.
I feel like those trees: between, neither.

Pulpwooders and landscape architects
have descended here.
They envision something more
than the apparent,
something with structure;
but they are the fools.

What can you say about someone
without secrets in these fields? About
someone who doesn't care
if everyone else knows all there is to know
about him? I wish I were
like that.

In our local feed-store parking lot
is a prisoner who nodded off
inside the prison van.
His dreams are more real
than his life has become;
he doesn't want to wake.

When the front door of my house opens
a bird flies in;
he sits upon the mantle for a while
until he decides to go.
Some would call it bad luck,
but must everything have a meaning?

Bestridden

There is a threshold in Texas
or Missouri
or Iowa
now, an edge where
taller green-ness of the East
turns short-scrub,
bluffed
to overlook westward
distant higher ground
that is
eventually tree-gone,
backlit by lightning. I'd like
to stand there a while,
look out, straddle geology
on
that
line.
If I wore side mirrors, I could
still look west and yet east
too, blinking back
and forth
eventually unable to distinguish
Fort Worth from Memphis
proper,
melding a bonsai version of the
continent
with huge
leafy then brown then browner
expanse.
Scribbled
on my palm
this point
is either the western or eastern
hem
of something. I would like to
tarry, grasp, then lose the map
so no one else could.

Bloomfield

On Christmas Eve
he'd come home
after eighteen hours' work
covered head to foot
in machine oil.
Old Broadway,
Macon,
yielded few jobs but these jobs
back in the Thirties:
the railroad
among the last
to give up men to soup lines.
He left
such things as presents
and cheer
strewn
because grind was all,
all was toil
was him.
The son, my father,
must have waited
patient
then distracted
for a returning
distracted
for some unity
humor and pursuit,
but waited too long
with Grandmother,
another stranger
to holiday.

Flood the Intersection with Bright, Bright Light

Flood the intersection
with bright, bright light
on shattered glass
showing sky-in-ground
more reflections than grains.

A mise en scene where spirits rise
a meeting of directions.
Something large
has happened here;
somewhere
empty houses.

The Ridgeline That Would Be Pine Mountain

(Above Barnesville, Georgia)

Tonight the ridgeline
that would be Pine Mountain
starts somewhere
north of Forsyth.
Hard spine,
oakwood and needles
all elevate around
nine hundred
then a thousand
then twelve hundred feet.
West of there
up on Hog Mountain,
years ago
Power Company men erected towers
to talk, listen, convey, warn, observe.
Not picturesque at all—
ratty even, preserved,
contradicting
a countryside lilted dogwooded delicate.

South southwest:
there is a culture of leaves
of hard men / soft women
of survivors
who lived died procreated
in shadows or openly
till all seasons
had passed.
The brush is scented
perfumed
with a cologne
that precedes us all,
that flows from their urges.
Here beaches once lapped
in delayed unison

left to right
west to east
depending on the shore's angle,
never quieted just receded
into sharkteeth
and sandstone
the shimmer
this life.

Adopted in McDonough,
abandoned
out near Johnstonville Road
now the dale in full slope
is a gathering of pine.
Marked stone with family
names repose at grove-edge.
Somehow distant trains
where no tracks were ever placed
sound tonight
in the air between here
and more quiet soundings;
embodiments
revelating us all
not fearing
the dead.
That skeleton of laughter
imprints
fall-line soil:
no crop allowed
to ever grow,
no root
to ever take.

Streamed, face down,
January rains find
a new cut
down gulfward 'round midnight.
Sweet jet fuel in the Flint River
cleansed
from proverbial fish--

Green Shoulders

no hook
can catch the past
no cast-across
no pond
can harvest what has gone.
Look up now to see
absence.
Even continents erode
waters having
no beginning
born not from sky
or lake
or springs.
And who can trace...sources?

Small portraits hang in the houses
below. Rooms are all that remain
pale green even ochre;
they reflect in gilded mirror
the flower petal veins.
Down under Hog Mountain
quail
sweet, plated and dim
have no powder burns
while placed on china.
Only wilderness scenes, remnants.
The light so different
sensation prismed
depending,
depending.
And south of Barnesville
on the road to Roberta
where clay-turns-sand
so remotely,
red tower lights
flash homing signals
bend echoes
bounce and fade
in Lamar County's
night air.

Even Nixon Could Change A Tire

Even Nixon could change a tire.
He told this to Chou En-lai
through his interpreter
in the Forbidden City,
nineteen seventy-two.
Snow-breaded grounds and statues
witnessed his admission
that winter day.
Dick could confess such simplicity
coyly self-deprecating, this being
the limit of his handiwork,
bounds of prowess.

Yet he couldn't
admit the quaking shadows
of Whittier even to himself...
they stretched across
his every tire track
upon dirt or pavement
traced to a troubled
awkward son, a figure
still under-axel
in an earlier California.

Luxeme

Reclining,
she transcends
the lime-colored couch
the red walls around
that disclose, they
mimic something just as red.
Her pout
hangs as she looks down
then up.
All of her words
have been edited
are perfect
with long soft shadows.

Things Left Behind

Not sure if it comforts or startles me
seeing the
abandoned
peeling house in Woolsey
with its flowers in full bloom:
vivid pinks, purples among nitrogen
that rise up to a broken banister, steps
and fallen oak.
It reminds me of things left behind,
like songs and poems
when the hand
has become potting-soil.

Rainy Season, June

Light green the bottle,
yellow chardonnay
casting sun-in-lime
along wall boards
wet now
with condensation,
fingerprints mar
the bottle's
coat of beads,
and I drink

drink to this rainy
afternoon
to this moment,
with only screen
to shield
the dripping
and wine to douse
my nakedness
all form fitted
teal.

Growing Season

With the hard freeze tonight
it signals an end to the growing season.
Winter mounts a countryside
weary and bare and strewn
with gentle bodies of deer,
upward-looking, eyes closed,
now collision scree. Roadside.
They will harden this evening
and as dawn approaches
a thaw cannot
until much later
until another springtide
releases dreams out of frozen heads
that will by then
be free to rot.

***The Heat of Blooming* (2008)**

The Heat of Blooming

Two birds,
prairie birds,
have wandered far
and ended up
here.

A mating pair,
chests as gold as a Kansas wash,
they are resigned
to arrival,
home now in the Flint valley.

O, how they must've
tumbled feverish
through storm, night
sighing all along
and off course;

the heat of blooming
can sometimes
make lovers
lose their
way.

Thomaston

I want to cut through steeps
like a river. Cut through a low ridge that
blocks all sources, so
the only way down to the Gulf
is straight through. And I
don't want to take eons, don't
want to pond before the heights and then
whittle away. The only answer for me
is hard water—explosive,
megatonic. I do realize, though, that once
the cut is made
my flow will settle
into a routine, and after the fall-line
I will just push sand aside
ultimately becoming level, wide, swimming
in myself, becoming something
that
remembers.

Cope

Sparks poured from a black bowl,
suns dividing like cells tonight
moving
above my acreage
quarantined here from all things day.
O sky time.
There is actually a hum emitted
massive
a rumble bigger than large,
featureless but for itself,
something without walls, so that
nothing stands
between me and.
and.

It's sky time.

Receiving Line

At the funeral in Ellaville
that little town among the fields
I stood in line for a forty-year-old man
never known to me, though I had known
his parents. He died by violence
in an unsolved crime.
While queued I avoided other faces
never knowing what to say. I smelled
liquor on someone's breath but
couldn't place
the brand.

***Torn Sky Bleeding Blue* (2010)**

We met in the Rothko Chapel

and I knew her by her
shimmer
afloat in the cool dark colors
along the lining of the room
without shape. She
enjoyed the paintings there,
said they were happy, said
they were smiling from
shadows.
But I couldn't be sure
what she meant. I couldn't see
the joy in those panels.
Then she was gone, as gone as
never.
And there I sat, stood
dreamed without sleeping.
I glowed like a nap.
Her perfume still
in that holy open space.

Arthur's Seat at Night
(Edinburgh, 1979)

On that windy hill
I felt
the city
flash.

Seas of the North
held my palms
combed my
hair.

Yellow lights, castles.
The Seat
in rock
blown.

For a moment
I was ancient
then I felt
my young face.

Gather Me

o gather me from the dead field
the one that lies before night
covers places where no one sleeps
or dreams or ever has

gather me there in a kind of ritual
and let me know this small moment
means more
than just harvest

stack me
on the border
of some greater
brightness.

***American Bruise* (2012)**

Leaves

Coming to rest, an American bruise,
Walt Whitman was already wringing out
his white beard in the brown waters
under a quarter-finished Washington steeple,
when morning arrived.
White coat soiled with blood and Maryland mud,
he hadn't been able to write much,
at least not during the war.

By then his Lincoln his Captain had ascended
the plains the bluffs the woods the farms of Illinois,
and Abe was green like a tree
by the time he'd arrived in Springfield to be buried.
Things were made to remain,but not people,
maybe not even words.

There is a later photograph of Walt in Camden,
of something scattered;
like winter smoke in a cobweb.

It's in black and white,
ink and paper, of course.

But death isn't the word
I'm looking for.

Lizella

Today I drove my father back to where he grew up
in Bibb and surrounding counties. He seemed to know
every house we passed:

"There's where Charlie Brown
and his beautiful daughters lived;
that's Dr. Holly's place;
Aunt Ida owned all the way to the corner;

remember this for me." There was a line, he told me,
a line where sand turns to clay.
It went through Grandfather's yard.

"We dug shark teeth from here," he said,
"three million years ago this was a beach,"
but I knew he meant three hundred million.

We drove along Sandy Point
near Echeconnee Creek
and his memory was whole.

The world was sienna.
"Just wonderful," he said.

Something Good has Come from Rotting

The old abbeys now in ruin
places without hymns or creed
their walls all that remain
of what has happened since those first minutes
then first days, months, decades, hundreds of years after the
preaching ceased.
No roof against the sky
no ceilings to shield rain from reaching
what used to be floor. I think those places are more holy now
with a view straight up
and into heaven. Something good has come from rotting,
shingles and beams no longer obstacles to infinity.
Decay has become the essence
of complete sacrifice.

Dead

My house breathes.
I can see it from the road.
There are dogs who wait
around it.

All life has drained from the cut hay
that no sun no water can resurrect.
It lies white, brittle, a remembered thing.

Worth more dead than alive
I drink wine on the porch.
I have trouble writing the word "dead."

Birds Won't Nest in the Sky

Some people paint their ceilings blue.
They say it's because birds won't nest
in the sky.

I would like to lie on a bed,
under such blueness, sapphire,
face up, lights out.

I'm sure stars would appear
there on the darkest nights.
They'd be gone by morning.

There is an ancient custom
from somewhere
about the depth of dreaming
when you have no roof.

The Viewing

A bourbon color and the sun blow my curtains.
I wait to go to the viewing.
They won't have music there.
They'll wait for the funeral to have singing.
But there's always a song in my head
when I wake, when I doze, drive, run, even dream.

A soundtrack is part of every scene.
That must be where my songs come from.

So there will be a song at the viewing after all,
a product of the self-taught, of the ear released
like a soul ascending.

Ray, with Tess

To Corey Mesler

They read Chekhov together
like it was the Bible. They
both knew, he and she,
that he was dying.
What a brave thing to do,
to cling to literature
as last rites, recited
over a body that lingers.
You see, he was a writer
and a writer understands
mortality. He allowed
a flow of a thousand birds
through his gills, inhaled
empathy through eyes,
skin. She
let him swim the flocks,
each feather a comb, each
word a comfort. And they
read. And the reading
became like mumbles
as he and she moved away
without moving, the text smooth
no vowels, no consonants.
Then she was alone, draped
in black, with a manuscript.
As she turned, looked out
of the window on the great river
the river where he caught his
wings, there were other fishermen
gathering, huddling
where it wouldn't rain.

Crazy

Ragged black clouds that can't rain.
What water they do produce trails only
part ways down. The air inhales it
far above ground. A shower dies
suspended, frozen like a hook.

I am really worried this time. In uncharted
country I pick up the pace, even
whistle this tune. I'm afraid
I might lose it all.
There are prayers I could say, prayers for morning.

My tune is a chain saw symphony with crickets, with fish,
with wrong way birds that can't read music.
All of this is home for me now. Like rain
that doesn't rain. They make mattresses specially
for rooms at the centers of houses to protect from

flying glass. From tornados. I sleep
on a mattress like that.

Along the River Road

Along the river road is the poverty
of love, of leaving everything behind
on some vacant weed-caked field
in a heat you didn't choose,
it's all here.

Alone in a culture of distraction
you make peace with your murder.
You swim.

Cousins Over Colder Fields (2013)

Ocmulgee Trio

Near the source of intermittent rivers

those butterflies again shoot across
wiregrass, droplets of autumn
caught in a headlight stream
a Gorecki moon beam.

No answers harvest
from dry watermarks but
there are sounds of the living
and remnants of the passed

old furniture antiqued and waiting
color—faded burgundy
and how will I explain all this
I wondered without resort to mathematics?

Safe passage

pale yellow west the sky
bespeaks strong white pine
and the music plays an old tune
I wrote in another life

when water was calm when
evening smeared the woods across
from everywhere the winds
and rains washed away sins.

Want you to know soon it'll dry out
and there'll be peace
moving through
so pray for safe passage.

She buried her mother today

in a coolish rain that spread
up from the Gulf.
Roads were muddy but

had been dry for too long
and it was the strangest thing
that two or three hours later

the sun came out as if for once
specified a green across gentleness
dotted the wet pine steeples

with bursting carpet.

Griffin

This time
I saw a bird
in the grocery store.
It was in Griffin,
it was July. Her
wings just wanted
air conditioning.
Now I ponder her reward.
I wonder if she's
still there tonight.

Monticello

I want to go
to Monticello,
climb that hill
and celebrate
my flaws,
swim
the renaissance,
look
west
to ideals
without
apologies
for never
having reached
them,
watch
the sun rise
from
the wrong side,
marry
woodlands,
drink
fine wine,
live a narrative
of liberty.

Wild Ravine

A Van Gogh,
described as such
being an article to some,
hung near a corner
of the large high ceilinged space.

I was the only one in front of it.
The room was sparse.
My breathing
just short of a pant.
My eyes watered.

The scene was a wild ravine,
whitewater frenzied.
I swear I heard him talking.

His misery right there
encased in medium.
He screamed. He shifted
turned moved, convulsed.

His expression
from my exact vantage
was panic.
The twisted strokes,
clenched teeth
crying "goddamn!"
with green-gray
white caked ghost blue

squirming swirled
over and over
    and
over and over.

The Salmon

I am he that is old
near rivers no one uses anymore

the deserted low country
breaks down when the past is all
if there were heads
there would be a memory
of water and green
and broken pottery

old pottery
slipped through
careless fingers

that once held
the stews of promise
sauces that got folks
through long pine shadows

of shrimp of sounds
of sleeping with golden sun
passing through oak leaves.

The river
already had his say
    careful
having cut through
thin watery empty ground.

Roseorange (2013)

Up Missouri

Somebody screamed out
Monk's name, but with-
out knowing the essence

of improv. It was New
Orleans without need to
blame anyone but herself

and it was right that she
typed instant prose
on an old Brother typeset;

the keyboard between her legs,
a cigarette hanging from
stubborn lips

damp in a sweat that
clocked the cold heart
of bad parenting

and the river a mile wide
by then, held tears
from nude Missouri widows.

Orson Welles Was a Liar

I have to write
something about him,
he the giant,
he the loser of cash.

His demonstration
of a point in space,
his lazar stare, his plans--
all were aeonian:

how he scraped together
just enough money
to fail at a project
enough for a story

to stay barely afloat
enough to start the next script and
enough for caviar
and other inspiration--

there's a special way
to lie that requires
talent and foresight---
not just anyone can do it.

Bill Evans

And he knew about deafening even in so-called places. From here I sense a brokenness a spiraling not quite against front and center, a falling that is wordless but with an open mouth, and a lack of interest as to where the piano lands. Those beautiful fat fingers.

It Rained on Resurrection Day

It rained on resurrection day.
The shadows that were limbs
against a white sky gave way
to what they would become.

There was a sense of gathering,
activity brimmed across
and onto fallen headstones
that were scattered in the brush.

Certainly nuns were singing out, and
they gave of their celibate-selves as
even the trees were wet with
an acceptance of circles.

Breaks

You'll notice the gap in my journal.
Though broken, it approached six weeks
or more. You'll wonder why the writing
stopped, slept, then awoke in time for itself.

There will be other questions, questions about
shadows and space and curtains that didn't move
even with windows cracked or open.

Later you will disregard the wondering altogether
and return to your moments,
your own moments of darkness and light.

But the break in my journal will still be there,
still with an open mouth that makes no sound.

Little Town gods (2016)

On This Side

Morning. And someone has
passed over the Jordan.
Going fast or leaving slow,
gone is gone. Listen.
Birds are living in the grove.
The ground below is a speckled
Gregorian checkerboard.

In the Clearing, A Shack

On the walls of a thousand ruins
is that blackening wood.
Suns cast on ivy doorways,
sweat, dry,
all leave kudzu poles
dotting the piedmont
with almost no memory
of Flovilla, Molena, or Butler,
Eatonton, or Warm Springs.
O ghosts who live in silvery
shacks, who ignore rights of way
and other lines—I apologize
for the language of idiots, but
never for the perfection of decay.

Like Kim Novak in *Vertigo*

she woke up covered with sky
and what water there was
filled the room where
she breathed. The bed kept her
for a while longer. The window
was open. Then with a force
of pure levitation, she slipped back
above the town.

Low Water

Outshoal slim
a black butterfly with
blue patches navigates
around our toiling
waning days under
ceiling fans, a world
non compos mentis
and in decline.

No use trying to convince
me against gathering
my own locusts
to combat the shade
crossing the Atlantic
from the left shoulder of Africa
every two dozen hours,
outshoal. Slow.

We hear October's voice
though what she says
sounds scrambled in a star-
burst of clear blue dry
patches fall sky,
and it moves shallow
dragonfly ridge clear eye
and it moves.

Outshoal soul
dry rocks in a cloudburst
wild and scenic and under
ground to nothing a powder
put in hot drinks
stirred combined ingested
and spat in a ritual
I'd thought we'd forgotten.

A Jerusalem of Ponds (2016)

Knowledge of Rooms

Flies the bird
through the old community building
a window opened at each end,
it's night out on a dirt road.

Knowledge of rooms
can save a life
the sparrow who renegotiates
when coming through

close to pews, benches
lamps, lecterns. In
the smell of broken pine
like an airliner

she's on course
down from high plateaux
where chapels, big houses
have only doors. Never ajar.

But through the breach
she's leaving. Onlookers
get the metaphor. But that bird
stays a pagan.

War

There is danger in jazz
danger in what
it lets,
in the envy it mothers
paying attention mostly
to how much a soul weighs.
These are times
of believing self-assurances
and sleeping at boundaries.
Jazz lets us do that. But now I
see lights in the woods.

Stork
to Glenn Gould

He used to be a friend
of mine in Toronto.

Someone said he didn't like
to talk, but sing. Not really

singing. And Bernstein
mentioned

his piano. I don't believe
Glenn would

know me now.
I think he walks alone,

his overcoat agonized
in self-pilgrimage.

He plays so late at night, he sings,
how can his parents sleep?

Macon, 1967

It was October. The front
room was full of people.
At that time older men
still wore hats when they
were dressed in their best

suits. This occasion was
a funeral. Conversation
was somewhat hushed
and there was food in
the kitchen where some

old women whispered.
There he sat well across
the room in a formal
gold padded chair. I
could smell the paper

mill. The sun came in
at an angle that lit only
his left shoulder and he
motioned for me to come
over. In that crowded

room he sat me in his lap
facing away and, placing
his hand upon my head,
my father cried
inconsolably.

Anxiety

The anxious
straddle tides
balance on rooftops
come and depart and
drop off and angle upwards
and derive from the odd
symptom or dark edge or a
night's clarity or a routine
or damned nothing.

The Killdeer Wheel

The killdeer wheel in plain
sight, like seabirds they
nest in the road with equinox
just beyond some trees.

La Mer plays on a device,
curtains billow in a March of
twenty-four-seven.
I put up

a fence of old cut timber
between me and a tall walnut,
planted dogwoods just behind
it. Losing topsoil at the speed

of slope of drop of scrub
the sea is where it
goes. Someday tree roots
will drain all piedmont lakes.

Digby Roundabout (2017)

Oconee

The pine-tree rolling's
a torn brown stocking
a rift that hugs the wing
curved ten miles all the way out
to the zero line. She used
to have names like
river lightning
or was called thunderstream
below hearing or
sound a water table makes.
But now she refuses a
name I can give.
Somebody sighs.
The rainflock sings again.

Funeral Road

Going down that funeral road
with signs from other times
essential remote obscuring frozen.
Even fields are England-reminiscent;
all pass through narrows there
rights of way made nighttime.
Pines overhang close-in over dirt
yellow darkened shortening evenday
lit only by some headlights' flood
under random weathered hemlock
turned longleaving.

Near the Lebanon

Turned in on herself she
this great half discus rains
here Persians used to walk Darien's
wideness here the ended Altamaha
opens onto Mediterranean straits
between Cyprus and Aleppo here

she wears strings wears fabric
innocent of coasts east of floods
stands near the high water washes down
a grey goose sky just visible up and out
where they've gathered dunes for hurricanes
barrier'd Cumberland peshmerga from
Jessup to Revelations.

The Road to Hamilton

There's an ethnicity of fields; they accompany
the way down to Hamilton.
Remainings line the road.
Crofts are mum like whippoorwills.
The effort that cleared them to the wood line
is so so gone. It still amazes me how shade
is jagged like endings and how living
is the hitch.

The Rainflock Sings Again (2019)

Ghost Over Woods

There's a ghost over the woods tonight.
He knows the dew point.
There's the music again. The unity.
I can only seed and cover with earth
a little rectangular swath, but he
gardens wherever it's morning.
Past the point, he dissipates to my
remaining.

Haralson

Reddish tint to blue-white spreads before it can find a clasping
disheartened from a rhythm of red clay
the streams calcify.

Chopin entertains a night of muted flashing dreams' refrain
he's frozen where ivory has a zip codex
a mind inlaid with butterflies.

The cut bank lines we make have staffs and sheets and quakes
unstilled fermenting but discolored now where the green was
and they say it evens.

The blue-black and east our evening molto roofless brick walls
fly without markings but for the planets
who eavesdrop.

Don't unsex my countryside of its dialect its greenery its truth be told
just leave alone the way that blood goes out
to all other matters.

Upriver Cloud to Cloud

She sings "Dust on the Bible"
at the overlook. The sun's
going down all orange
in polite but scattered
applause. Someone should
paint this.

A storm rakes
upriver cloud to cloud;
it's only backdrop because
it'll die out
long before getting this far west.
The next one I think she wrote.

Her songs
reach conclusions.
They are gathered they resemble
birds and geography. Frontiers
blend into zones and then open
space she sings something like
a sparrow that's fallen.

In an Effort to Fly

Skim low the waters
just above a wake
great orange cotton
out in the eastern frame.

I could be a finch
with gold on my shirt
I could recite some words
in an effort to fly.

The wing and the anti-wing
the gill and its other
succumb to solar wind
I write names on my hand.

To know that kind of happy
careless but for breathing
I could have ponds for shoes
and a hat made of whistling.

Move

The twenty third of the month
and hundreds of cranes
from Sand Hill
move.

Breathing flush with steam
the great rainflock sings
shaming more starlings
than I can count.

A status quo sopping
they fly they skim through
cloud bottoms gray and heavy
and north pointed.

Sound a migrance.
I've counted half a thousand
in ten minutes. The green air
remembers just ahead of raining.

They're in Sharpsburg by now;
frequency
goes quiet.
Then showers.

Floodlit (2019)

Mornings at My Angkor Wat

Few places won't yield to sky.
But these wide massive stands
confront almost any godhead.

The interior has little solid floor
unless you count canopies
given way to great leas.

Sometimes a dry-season patch
can expose a thirty-mile view.

Still, what hard vantage

the night gives. Even out here a glow.
I'd like to cut the feed. To shut down
the juice. And just be.

Holed-up for good, mornings
at my Angkor Wat would make
a home here along the seldom roads

where I'd charge for admission to myself
so I can pay me back all the things
I've lost.

Shallows, Walking

I.

The snow's almost gone now.
The ground rises to meet both oaks.
Dotted white their hidden sides
are shadows pouring out across
our floor. Look at my hands my feet,
they're ragged. I prefer low sun

to cold and places south to north.
The benevolent Gulf. Even from here
I feel those shallows.

II.

There's a thought I have about
walking the property in each
of the seasons. I'd sit on the marble bench
in its almost-room, walls of branches
a grotto-place where deer sleep.
Then I'd walk the path around periphery
and see it leads back to me. The me
who walks here only after
I leave.

The Return

Rain again. The back planks are a sponge.
Out behind the house and down some steps
there's the return from whence it came.

Low ceilings over a field of robins. They look up,
equidistant to the dance. They seem astonished.

More raining. Harder now. It pools a world
then slopes away to sea, all the while greeting
those of us who swim. Joined to everything
that's round, we move together in radar-red

formation. We fly.

Where the Five Counties Meet

this countryside catches
blurred veils
moving curtains of rain
almost silent across
tops of trees and clearings
and up to the house.

My god at the time, the clouds
my god at the lake, the face
I only know at a distance.

The west gives birth.
A breeze begins. My old gilded
book quivers on the front porch.

I know the way out-past the fences
but here is a place. Sounds
like showers fill the woods
long after they've passed over.
I ignore the rustling approach.
Then I count to one.

A Great Wheel Thunders

A great wheel thunders
in the attic. Such
a bringing forth of blooms.
Morning crackles new
mourns a reason to even be.
And miles-long sheets
of tin unflag, they rattle
in response to
happening at all.
The procession inside

that living that flash
rolls to somewhere else
and never here long enough
to call it staying.

Breathing Through Planks

Wind yes the songs of wood and
walls and cypress swamp the lungs
breathe through planks so hard as to
cast off nails that try to pierce
countless coats of red then white
then brown then forest green
sloped away from the rest of the house
for when rainy seasons hit again
when the clouds need somewhere to go
sound with artifacts with layers

below street level between words
and memory where notes, letters end
where there's quiet
in this noisy head.

Water Lily

She walks through the grove
under high ceilings. It rains
and augments change, clings
like a sweet-onion bloom.
She fixes eyes on the narrator.
The source of children sways
backlit, immersed by intinction.
Eternal.

The Leaving Part

And in the morning
there's the leaving part,
a quiet pull and turn
that makes the past

of a place. Again
this empty house when
no one's here
laments

the vacuum from
a door that's closed.
A going but
not a letting go.

John Bell Hood

rides the cross-tie line
along what would be Highway 41
to Lovejoy to red clay.
He's full of porcelain thumbs
his bible folds his ghost
petrified red scar gone blue.
The Texas song re-loops
a weeknight from his youth.
A glow shows he's lost an eye
a glass half full of limbs.

Floridita

Small green rooms. Large space. The doorknobs are no
match for an ocean twenty miles west of this old river-house.

It sits half a block off the channel and feels the pull from
the only moon we've ever known. In the morning she

finds her voice again in sweet-water springs now black with
buried leaves. Only a few walls of the Tamiami

persuasion survive along highway Forty-One where even rust
leaves for home. But from a thousand hinges, tacks

and the rubble of a pulled-down garage on the property line
comes a bloom.

The Torn Screen

The torn screen had been tacked with a nail
so as not to flap in breezes from out-east
that convulse in petit mals
over this great fronded hammock.

So I tacked it again. But it couldn't hold,
refusing to be a filter just a filter,
preferring width over being a wall of points
between metal threads.

Maybe I feared birds coming onto the porch.
Maybe I feared my own flight the other way
through and out into the world. Maybe I feared
death.

A final time I tried, even placing a tile
against its lagniappe fringe to help
the small nail head catch and hold back
the wind with a tatter.

Still it winked for a time then became
a flag again, its tiny holes a mockery
of a door a window a pass that opens
to a gulf of whatever comes next
and next.

The Flats

The road between Monticello
and Yankeetown rolls empty
like the sea level woods that crowd it.

Even in the day you drive with head-
lights on as not to wing a deer, hawk,
Chevy truck or distracted hat.

On one stretch there's nobody, the big
bend just beyond. So at night it's no

place to be.

Way off you can see the cooling towers:
two floodlit steaming sea cows who watch,
their eyes just above tide.

A few miles in, the blacktop cools
but not enough to use the passing lane.
And all side roads have no turnarounds.

Those on the right find water. Taillights
are red stars miles ahead. Tonight
they fade like the reasons they came.

Storm Over Three-Forks

In great creases of night
waters fall to the coast.
Sometimes a face or stone
will rise after dark
like a skull or soul
in the channel,
his forehead pointing
to curtained stars
inside an x-ray bright
nightish sky.
Then that stranger will ride
blackened chutes
flashed into life by
storms over Three-Forks
continuous, so distant
they're quiet,
sound gone before
they're heard
but seen and pressed there
between mountain thighs
tethered now down
to the level of seas.

Smarr

The small town of Roberta half-smiled
through its west-facing broken-glass windows
and looked out on a gray
summer soup.

I was taking my father through
the county's second city, second to
its abandoned county-seat, Knoxville.
Now in his ninetieth year, he had no idea

we were in his old places of course,
but I drove down to Macon in a half-circle
by way of Barnesville, Roberta then Lizella,
just to do it

again. And it tried to rain but couldn't.
The sky strained for any fall
but it was frozen
in July veneer.

Later we stood in line for lunch
over on Riverside Drive. Daddy
asked a stranger, is this Mercer?
The man replied, no it's the S&S.

It was on the way home
as we passed through Smarr
that it finally rained, making rivulets
along a wide open highway Forty-One.

I imagined
the rain would soon know
the taste of salt as it had before
again.

Tranquility Base

It was July 1969 down on Lake Sinclair.
Outside was a night as loud as Mombasa.
Inside the astronauts came down a blurry
black and white ladder, likewise the old TV.

My crewcut years then at ten were just
a clutching of books near
two-hundred-year-old nesting-oaks.
I lurked at the edge of reddish water
and miles-dark hardwood

under yin/yang skies. Later in that cabin
I tried to sleep maybe channel astronaut
dreams, but settled on the hawk
dreaming floodlit over the boathouse,
her shadow pouring out to find me.

A Sky-Wide Russet Flock Ascending

Before sunset but just
through the terraced clouds of a dusty month
and no rain since the hurricane,
end-time trumpets rise from local ponds
along the fall-line.

Since the fires of singularity up to now,
when that leaving shines through rows
of sibling pine and random skeleton
oaks, veterans from an oxbow creek

risen in the sun's departure

streak orange under blue and
onto a thousand mirrors
flashing a sky-wide
russet flock
ascending.

The Width of Here (2021)

Your Breathing

Here, leaning-in
to get a better
view

I think while sunning
full-faced, there's
poignance

in my brevity.
Truth shows up.
The metal's edge

makes a cicatrice
of a once-clean place.
Geography rises

then breathes out.
Perfume on my hands,
Arabian,

can't distract from
the tattoo that is
my room.

I join your breathing.
It teems.
It crowds.

Unanimity

Redwings pour out from
any number of trees
a formation, a singularity
then a sky. They crowd
the edges, a few drops
but holding,

brimming
not straying away from
the local common lung
and comforted in their
unanimity like a thermal
black flag cast into weather.

All of Our Living

There's a jumping between trees
a slight elevation luring wings
across, along, among.

A refusal to cede a greening
back to gray becomes part of me.

Catching my breath
just after pneumonia,
I glide, I see

the air the sky holds all of our living
holds me and my chatter, holds you.

Miller's Thumb

I.

How deep is the green skin
out to the east and away
into wideness?

Aerial shots taken without
consent show just how
alone we are.

And nobody said anything
about consequences.
So, no escape this time.

We're known by
our remaining, not
how we arrive.

II.

Pages don't turn
they're burned.

Be careful what
you fish for. You

could kill it. And poets
are the first to go.

Riddle me the weight
of civilization.

But scales vary
with the miller's thumb.

Between Butler and Columbus

Late. Red.
Thunderhead-soaked sundown
almost a whole county wide
in an otherwise
purple clarity.

Not from radar but conveyed
through dead-reckoning
and Kentucky windage
a blood colored marble range,
its innards flashing pregnant.

Due south,
its base hidden by the curve,
is the great churn with
outer walls of veined lightning
a full eighty miles away.

Halo

This butterfly
in a moment of showers,
a devil-beats-his-wife,
seeks the magnolia sheen,
a siren, a bloom
like a lighthouse.
She treads the smaller
thermals, part of a halo
encircling all trees.

Le Papillon, she dries
what beads remain
with brightness, a self-made
fan. But then again, her torn sky
bleeding blue into fields,
a bruise the size of weather
sheet-flows, and she finds
shelter, overgrown, there—
yellow, black, wet
at rest.

Portion

Just like a Jain, I'm careful to step
where nothing else is, and when I feel
something under my foot I lean away
I try, while going.

My portion parades like screenplay
up to now and now and again I relate it all
to sparrows; they fly near the eyes of
my passing through.

Conversation with Rothko

Red

The world is not a kind world.
It's best to realize this.

Red doesn't occur in nature;
we seek it through our fear of red.

Colors are ghosts of bone-houses
gone now to seed.

Blue

The opposite of windows is the
open air.

Darkness in the foreground makes
alive the western skies.

And wind can give texture to things
that cannot, will not move.

Green

I had wished to hold a moment,
an aerial view of the counties.

Death is peace, water flows
uphill and clocks aren't veined.

We can count to nothing and start again,
or else become the leaves that we are.

Black

A magnet for vision draws-in all eyes
and itself and sings.

One is one is none is everything but
even light can't escape.

Unsex the sunset, take it to
the perfect night of prayer.

White

Painters have nothing to say anymore,
they flood the intersection with bright

bright light, play God,
make holy the vacant.

I walk out of the chapel into a glaring
absence.

Yellow

There is no yellow in point of fact; it's only
suggested by an empty width out before us.

Don't offer heat to the cold morning,
add nothing, remain, stop your painting.

But we aren't at home here.
Otherwise we would just breathe.

New Poems

2022-2023

Green Shoulders

After a Few Wet Months

A giant stream of redwings, grackles
they cross my winter field from woods
and seem to empty out into openness
     spill like creeks to a sea
     sweep through small gaps
and carbonate the sky.

Across across. They light. We light.
And after a few wet months the cold
is more acute. My walks around are
full of blow-down timber just prior
to breathing dreams of a later
     green.

The world is too loud now
except in the coves, the grottos
the edges of reds, indigos,
deepest of blues
the cavernous thicket
     covers me

while those birds
hang like leaves above
then flash to-ground, rise like
black steam and scatter sun
across their boiling backs onto a house,
its white wall pocked by a million
     thoughts in that single shadow.

Sunrise, Late Winter

About halfway past seven just as
the northeast sky lit up orange
from waters aloft

      I looked right and, distracted,
      thought of all those million souls
      then flying in waves

towards Carolina, paper fragments,
moments though scattered still clamoring
for a snuffing-out like flocks of keys

      from pianos or like escaped moths
      bee-lined to the truth they know
      and received only by such light.

Pastoral (January)

Wet, old, eastern land stretches
out and over a slope;
it evokes a breathing-out.

The ground is shadow-full
buried shallow under bottomlands
exposed by rains
shown in walls of little gorges
recent, red, disheveled,
a witness to orogeny.

Layers well acquainted with weather
now minuet along highway-sixteen
road cuts below three-sixty views
of easy green without
divertimento.

Slow-Burn Sky

A landscape view, but sky
takes up three-fourths
of the sweep.

A slow-burn pit—its A-shapes
of variously named oak—looks
resigned here.

I've placed fragments around
the ring—old quartz, granite
unmoved

by my brevity—they yawn
at eons, sleep through
spans.

Still I live longer than now
still burn under
my skin, clothes.

I leave few remnants, carve
nothing that lasts, char only
paper

in pursuit of pyrrhic gestures
not to gods but to angled light
that only sunsets give

for whatever reason
whatever reason else
I can't imagine.

Beyond the Fire Pit

Where clippings go
    burned, piled, compiled
long shadows now lean
into the east.

Gaps between wooden
planks lead up to a barn
    full of growing
like it will never freeze.

There must be a plan
a point to activity
all the flexing, tensing
    all the going.

Red wings become carpet—
disturb the winter ground
light on ideals of one mind
    but miss their target
        with smoldering
        intent.

Current

Cold veins of weather
rotate, they twirl and
bounce and may want to
    avoid my seeing
them but I see

those fingers gesture
my direction while
another hand behind
holds a playing card
    of me.

With all this talk of snow
forever north of here
never passing
    from almost
    to comes-a-time

now deep-frozen
I'm placed on burnt edges
    of certain fording
the great river
we reach—

there at the mouth a gulf
blue as cobalt, white as a sun
my current flows a deep-field
between all possible infinite
    compass points

then this—the aging
from first motion up to here
disturbs my status, my quo
the top of my pond across
    and distracts what
could be a fount.

Tonnage on the Rivers

Refusing to die
without living,
I and the sky
fly so blue as
to not be blue

while the planet tilts
and takes me with it
grinding, crawling
to southernmost solstice.

This world creaks
like a wooden ship
spread across pasturage
heretofore reserved for

    quiet

and its kin.

As creeks find the easy way down
they confuse me as to whether
the crease or the water
came first

like tonnage on the rivers
they sleep above fall-lines
wait, prepare
for the risen spring still far
over the south horizon

and pocked by great
flocks of starlings
who ask
what is freedom
if I choose
slavery?

Kneel the Cattle

Under winter lightning kneel the cattle
while behind windows
    I bathe in a flashing room.

Dreams of sea-level fill thunderheads:
they drain all darkness down to the Gulf.
Their song rattles windows
    hereabouts.

Someday I'll die too
on a course to later fall as rain
when the cedars bend
and the air changes just
enough—then the number 'one'
will
share me
with about
    a billion stars.

Older Fields

The story in my head
is real. I cannot
write it down.

A red star swerves
across fields older than
I can ever paint

as a winter sky calls me by
a name my children knew,
and so be it.

My spine arches
at the pain Mother shows.
But I am late.

Almost-Full Moon Through Branches

The almost-full moon chatters
through a bone-house of oak
in the front clearing,

This property is filled
with hardwood, cedar, pine
holding back fully open views

during the hard season
long before a last frost
and its unfathomed harvest.

So runs the talk of war:
it quivers like smallish woods or a pond,
distorts like an old torn speaker.

What appears behind branches
only validates the ear of counsel
as now all concord breaks.

Still

A short memory of winter
like childbirth they say
sustains this oval year.

A sleeping tree peers
through window-frost
still scares the children

but so-what to icy winds:
they'll soon wither
at the sight of July.

That's when the water
barely
moves.

The Usual Path of Cranes

Violins combine to present
a full wall of anxiety
but as background deep background
like a middlemarch sun sloped
in slow loops ever softer north
the little mandolins skim the pond
in welcome

and when people say those seasons
change according to a linear way
tell them I feel that slow veil
lifting from all points
filling the air with ghosts
a barking of dogs and herons
who've chosen not to follow
the usual path of cranes.

Another Springing-Forth

July drones, but no voices
are heard except ones
from December that wait
below ground, wait for
the later times to emerge
and become more than
a way remembered but
a new way from
these hardened fields.

The front door opens to great
heat and a realization
of how our homes breathe
even long after they become
ruins, all in advance and
beyond at the same time,
layers like rock, sand,
bones and oil that comprise
and complete us.

And when the cold comes,
when the quiet envelops
where decibels once flowed
from the soul's tenancy,
it startles to know what
the world before and after
really takes, uses, eats, drinks
all as sacrament
for yet another springing-forth.

The Ibis Returns

and somehow I sleep
first in an oak then down
to shallows for the fish
lulled indifferent under
cover dreams between
around water plants in
angled pollen-hazed
waning light.

Yellow Butterflies Return

Yellow butterflies return
    to oaks in the grove.
They accompany a landscape
    gone to seed, ragged
and wet in the sunlight.

Their coming signals
    a betweenness, something
in-wait and resistant to linear
    time-framing with blinders,
the view right-now.

We can't hear
    concussions erupt across
other fields and parking lots—
    but here small membranous
wings become
beautiful debris.

A Birdshadow Drones This Low Country

where the water is up
and discards the edge of
sky for stone. Shards
of night take to heaven, join
old ground, cast across farms
that used to be closer to
each other.

And yet I hear whispers
from way-across valleys tilled
by weather and a passage of names
seemingly living but that somehow
fail the try, all the while detached
in dis-memory of any familiar
face or fee-simple border.

Home when it's night, loss when
all sight has left from the wait
of a people promised their roots
but, undelivered, endure our pastures
culled of all but their county seats
and mouthing some words
off the by-God record.

Most of these roads tend east to west
or square corners like math, angles
too sharp for telling a truth except
in the presence of ghosts
who point like compasses schooled
in all but direction.

There go the birdshadow paths their
contrails bereft their afterbirth held up
as yesternight's template, they leave
a gnawance verging on dust with
clarity so distinct as to alarm all
watchers and repel sanity when
sanity's so much needed now.

Above and Over

Above and over the evenings of spring
the steams of change obscure ridgelines
down to a merge, forgetting
the difference between rivers
and blood.

O the sun slips as do the empires
with sounds of pester and frenzy;
as quiet overtakes the amber line
preceding flashes that will follow.

Towers rattle waist-deep in tabby;
they wade in what comes
with a focus on self as opposed to others,
thus breaking the most important
of all commandments.

The Light that Travels

On this morning that seeps then pours
into bright halls, through small rooms
woods, over shoals, shallow bays
and floods the seaboard streams
    and grasses, expands rocks
      at their highest points,

I continue into what unfolds
    like
geologic
time
with its low groans and
scraping and cracks
in a godhead flow
I can only ride
and not divert.

The Planets

There, all in a line and just above
    Christmas lights
near cedar and bare-bone oak—
the planets.

Slight off-center to the greatest
    disk
one in a trillion but still one by-god
our galaxy.

And a looming white-pocked cheese
    seems in labor to the east,
it opens and closes like an eye
strung along behind.

All of us cling to dice cast before
    a blue wall
daily under wraps till this night
comes again.

Because when the sun goes
    we'll all go with it
all we've read or said will dissipate
to rise in some other way.

Sunlight From a High Window

shows on the onion
I am cutting.
The serrated verge
and a truth

peel away through skin
by way of red clay flowing
until the spleen shines

and to the knife

gives way.

A Dove's on the Roof

Words between the words,
a dove's on the roof.

Clouds show ragged
and dark south of here and
no music plays from the passing
cars.

Someone whispers about secret
police, the choosing of sides, of trees
stripped bare from artillery and art
that missed the mark.

We loiter
against the posting of signs while
behind is always in the present
tense,

mindful under pouring
rain, splayed as a public
watches.

So Change the Doves

The countryside wills a spring collected from
all rain barrels for miles around,
and its prayer congregates in details edging
open spaces just at the treelines

with movement in the groves again
and bushes full of wings
like brushes dipped in paint
searching for a sky.

The fact of happening every time can't take
this shine away. So change the doves
in creek-bed songs, they pond and fill a greenery
and rustle next to houses.

That Massif in the Room

I.

Woods in post-bloom bristle and sway
slow draws through-over-around
each a perfect perch

with just beyond more of the same
a series of infinitely small moments
further halved

never quite to a stop, a sad reticence
at cessation always blazing new ways
to that massif in the room.

II.

The other night after three AM
a bird sang from the bushes
outside a window full-throated
in pitch black, filled, embedded
there I think he was jonesing for
sunrise.

Like a monastery bell at vespers
a candle, the bird only hinted
never told outright a guarantee
of another rotation and then
I realized we were both awake.

Where I Planted Trees

some took root and have joined
shadows of the other ones.
They contemplate sky,
    later
    a path.

Then again
the blow-downs
die of fright
at the hems of open field
they face, before long
succumbing to such
    width.

I wonder at the grove
at its weeding-out the old
for the more recent and
I see myself early and late
    and there.

The World Breathes Out

Dry but soft, the world breathes out
angled light that's panned from
piedmont shallows. It looks like
the shiny side

of the mirror, no song
but wrens
and a weather-vein wind-mill.
Cessnas drone like
     a cello sputters

across an eastern sky dry but
soft
in gilded air
with green shoulders,
there

a jet path won't stir the porch;
burning
tires or trains can't break
indifferent fields
or me

or anybody else. But this is
what
gold comes from, and
where
venison runs
right through.

Shake and Flash

The plants hear thunder
feel the woods shake and flash
in those rains preceding
a warmer season

a frenzy
like the first frenzy
soaked down to essence
and the womb.

Along the Line

Morning flutters
along the line.

The stirs the flashes
call flocks of me
my consonants
call the light crested
through and between
leaf-clusters
still wet with prints.

It's hard to halt
a moment
hard to breathe
disturbance
hard to leave
when everything
leaves.

The Pond is Low

That Ibis is gray against
powder blue to white
alone and beyond
the roof now.

His trajectory makes
an arc away and over
some pines in remission
from summer.

The pond is low. Somewhere
but not here the world
the storm, there lightning
fills a sky.

An equinox glow evens
to sounds below hearing
for the last wing leaving
dead oak creek.

How a Painting Sings the Rainshadow Song

I.

That's twice a teenage red-tail buzzed me,
such close flying, even once with a hawklet
out from thickets through scattered new pines
then over the pond—all with no sound,
only what little wind there was.

For not even a second a flashed image there
gave a wisp of one of the southeastern tribes
red clay people like hawks turned to profile
showing a willingness to pounce if anything
moves within a hundred miles, patterns woven
into wings, and motion, and thermals.

II.

A soul housed in plumage tilts on a clifftop now
soft as its hardened face is not. Tears ride no
arroyos but bead like wine on blue acrylic
a fall-line above sandy fields when light
becomes smaller and sighs a veil.

A word for this, much less these, could
sew shut the speaker's mouth, or make
a non-stop rainshadow song while
just over the hill storms never
end their raging,
or sparks the russet-feathered
memory of the totality
of all knowledge being
snuffed by a great cull.

More Like Breathing Than Rain

I.

Who played that song
that night—
the one out by the beach
in air caked by dinner time
and rain more like breathing
     than rain?

II.

The woods are bare here now
but warm air streams up
from a gulf once and future and
the rain's more like
breathing
     than rain.

III.

I ride the past like
a saddle half in shadow
no other reference point
but rain, more like
breathing
     than rain.

Matte

A white matte of clouds
as if behind wax paper screens
moves slow across the sky
like a flock in the atrium
of immense holy space—
determined
though fearful,
proceeding
though paralyzed
from events.
Foreground and distance
combine into
something
imminent, terrible,
completed.

The Unused Gate

    The originals
high above they swirl
an hour or so
either side of dusk—
those icons
    in their gloaming.

    A crescent trails Jupiter
bright and over a twenty-year
evergreen placed not planted
    under that loud dark'ning.

    Southwesterly
a rose-orange sky boils at the gate;
it's always open now seized-up
overgrown never to swing
to scratch clay or make an arc
    no more purpose.

    Nearby
a mature wing sees me. He's
brown and white and heaving
perched on the bones of april
beside what's become
    a gap in the fence

    he gestures me
something about great ovals
like blades that slice
an ever-thinning
    minute.

    Utterly still but orbiting
the old hawk settles
at buddha-gate
    in instant
    halted
    velocity.

There Since One of the Wars

Red from the east shone
on a house's white side
there since one of the wars
it waits for rain.

Someone stands in a second
floor window, the glass fogged
to obscure
what more weather will hide.

The pane is old too.
It imitates that bloody sky,
reminds of evening, dim
like the last breath of strangers.

No sailors to caution us
or weathermen to warn but
this is not a drill they say
this is not a drill.

The Good and the Gone-to-Seed

Water won't allow a lake for long
before the river
breathes again.

Ruins watch us, weathered, by now
only bones: no roof, no
catch-basin barrel, just windows
and doorways to a gulf below.

But it still rains on both the good
and the gone-to-seed
as one true equity.

Cartographer

I.

On the walls,
door frame to sill to
window to corner and then
again, are topo maps their smallish
lines that somehow follow shades
blended into bold edges long and
bordered with green-brown lighter
to night-like loud
whispering.

II.

I think I'm obsessed
when it comes to those maps,
resolved but not resigned
to letter forms, some with
Latin roots draping over steps,
drop-offs onto even wider plains
and smaller clustered right-angled
signs of intent.

III.

If I've missed something
through my focus on detail or
its other, then it's on me—
my zeroed-in standing-back has
taken me away or zoomed me
towards, while my purpose begins
or has begun to elude or render
anything not plotted by degrees
of east west north south
as meritless.

Wednesday

From whom all blessings flow
comes the sound of streams
and rain and flashes
and that which is allowed
in a breeze or pyroclasm
barely moves a strand of hair
except as truth.

To think all-in-all is hard
but to receive it can seem
impossible, like seeing
the universe through a needle's door
or a sky shown in shards of glass.
And being alone—

alone only as it means
singularity, means complete,
means the sum of one and none.
And that noise sparks utter
silence. And that silence
is a bell.

A Storm Out to the East

looks even more so
with sunset opposite

casting big light. It burns
red to blue to black

as if rain could spark
a chain of thunderheads

and end all talk
of concord.

Green Shoulders

www.ingramcontent.com/pod-product-compliance
Lightning Source LLC
Chambersburg PA
CBHW071352080526
44587CB00017B/3066